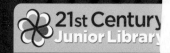

21st Century
Junior Library

MW01222305

MAKING A DIFFERENCE WITH EASTERSEALS

easterseals

Beth Finke

How Can I Help?

Published in the United States of America by:

CHERRY LAKE PRESS
Ann Arbor, Michigan
www.cherrylakepress.com

Reading Adviser: Beth Walker Gambro, MS, Ed., Reading Consultant, Yorkville, IL
Photo Credits: © kali9/iStock.com, cover, title page; Courtesy of the Columbus Metropolitan
Library Digital Collections, 5, 6; Nixon White House Photographs, National Archives and
Records Administration via Wikimedia Commons, public domain, 8; Library of Congress,
National Photo Company Collection, 10; © Easterseals MORC, 12, 14, 21; © Jordan Strauss/
Invision/ASSOCIATED PRESS, 18; © ACHPF/Shutterstock, 20

Cherry Lake Press is an imprint of Cherry Lake Publishing Group.

Library of Congress Cataloging-in-Publication Data has been filed and is at catalog.loc.gov.

Cherry Lake Publishing Group would like to acknowledge the work of the Partnership for 21st
Century Learning, a Network of Battelle for Kids. Please visit Battelle for Kids online for more
information.

Printed in the United States of America

Note from publisher: Websites change regularly, and their future contents are outside of our
control. Supervise children when conducting any recommended online searches for extended
learning opportunities.

CONTENTS

TRAGEDY LEADS TO INSPIRATION

In 1907, Homer Allen had just graduated high school. He was out celebrating. He was riding a streetcar in his hometown of Elyria, Ohio. His streetcar crashed, and Homer and eight other people were badly injured. He lost his legs. Elyria was a small town and did not have a hospital. Homer could not get help.

An early 20th century streetcar in downtown Elyria, Ohio

Homer's father, Edgar Allen, was devastated. Elyria needed better hospitals. Injured and disabled children needed better care. Edgar Allen did not want other families to suffer. He asked people to donate and was able to raise a lot of money.

Edgar Allen opened a hospital for disabled children. And that was just the beginning.

Edgar Allen created a national organization to support disabled children. In the spring of 1934, they started selling stickers to raise money. Each sticker cost one penny.

The Elyria Memorial Hospital was built in 1908 in response to the streetcar tragedy.

Look!

Look at the picture on page 5. How is it different than a city today? How do you think life might have been harder for people with disabilities in the past?

Donors stuck them on envelopes and letters to show support for the cause.

The stickers (or postage "seals") became popular all over the United States, especially around Easter time. That is why they named the national organization Easterseals. Easterseals centers were opened across the country. These centers didn't just help children. People of all ages with disabilities came to Easterseals centers for services. Many people found jobs at those centers, too.

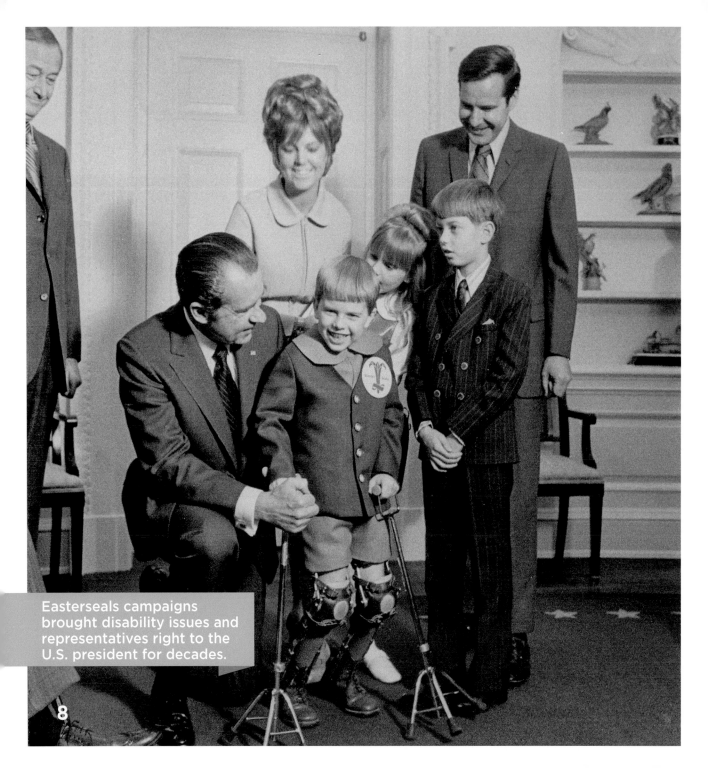

Easterseals campaigns brought disability issues and representatives right to the U.S. president for decades.

BUILDING A MORE INCLUSIVE WORLD

Before Edgar Allen started Easterseals, the world was not very accessible to people with disabilities. Street corners didn't have curb cuts for wheelchairs. Blind children weren't taught Braille in school. In fact, children with disabilities were often not allowed to go to school at all. Schools did not have wheelchair ramps. Streetcars and trains didn't have lifts.

Even doorways and public restrooms weren't wide enough for wheelchair users.

In an **inaccessible** world, children and adults with disabilities often stayed home. Neighbors never saw them. People had no idea how many millions of Americans had disabilities. They didn't know about

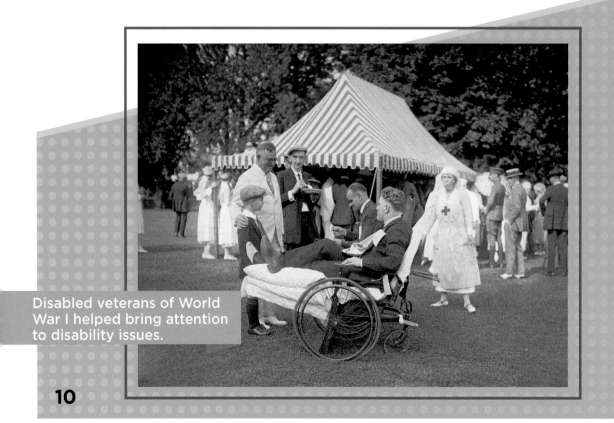

Disabled veterans of World War I helped bring attention to disability issues.

Think!

What would life be like if you weren't allowed to go to school with your friends?

all the things people with disabilities are able—and want—to do.

People with disabilities enjoy the same sorts of things everyone else does. Sometimes they just need "helping tools" like ramps to get into and out of buildings, push buttons to open doors, Braille to read books, American Sign Language (ASL) to communicate, and wide doorways for wheelchairs, among other things.

Providing accessible opportunities for fun and community connection is an important part of Easterseals' work.

Make a Guess!

When do you think disabled children were guaranteed the right to go to school? If you guessed 1990, you're right! The Americans with Disabilities Act (ADA) of 1990 guarantees disabled children the right to an education.

Easterseals has spent nearly 100 years working to make the world more accessible. They provide education, transportation, and job training. They advocate for accessibility. They provide services in homes and in communities. They provide day camps and sports leagues. They work to help people with disabilities and their families live full and independent lives.

Easterseals empowers families and helps strengthen the disability community.

14

Ask Questions!

Ask a teacher, librarian, or other adult about what kinds of assistive technology they have or know about. Ask if that person can teach you how it works.

One in every four people in the United States has a disability. That includes over 3 million children. Helping disabled people and their families is so important. Easterseals helps families get access to the right care. Families can learn new skills together and enjoy fun activities with an inclusive community.

EASTERSEALS NOW

Easterseals has grown! Today, Easterseals has disability services at centers all over the country. People with any disability, including those who need mental health services, can find help at Easterseals.

Easterseals programs are as diverse as the people they serve. There are programs to help teach children and adults how to use assistive technology. Some programs teach people with disabilities, older workers, and veterans new job skills to find paid work. Easterseals also

Make a Guess!

works to help autistic individuals and their families meet their life goals.

Easterseals centers today provide physical and occupational therapy for disabled people. They also offer recreational programs like sports leagues. Adults and children can make new friends, relax, and have fun.

Easterseals works to make sure everyone is included and respected—at home, in school, and out in the community. They also want to show that disabled people belong on TV and in movies.

Actor, comedian, and filmmaker Nic Novicki launched the Film Challenge in 2014.

Think!

How does having more disabled people in movies and TV help the disability community? Why do you think it is important that disability stories get told?

That is why they collaborated with Nic Novicki, the founder of Easterseals Disability Film Challenge. Every year, people with and without disabilities come together to make short movies about disability in its many forms. Winners receive support and opportunities to meet people that can help their career in entertainment.

With access and opportunity,
all people can thrive.

We can all find ways to be more inclusive and make sure everyone feels they belong—because they do!

How can you help make a more inclusive world? Learn more about disability, whether from books like this or ones in your school library. Treat disabled people with the same respect you would want to be treated with yourself.

Create!

Create a list of ways you and your friends could support Easterseals and its services in your community. Maybe you could design your own seals or a poster to help spread the word!

GLOSSARY

accessible (ek- SEH-suh-buhl) open and able to be reached without obstacles

advocate (AD-vuh-kayt) to defend or promote a cause or idea

assistive technology (uh-SIH-stiv tek-NAH-luh-jee) a device or program that can help a disabled person interact with and navigate their environment

Braille (BRAYL) a system of writing created with raised dots used by blind and visually-impaired people

disabled (dis-AY-buld) to have a physical, mental, cognitive, or developmental limitation

disabilities (dis-uh-BIL-uh-teez) physical, mental, cognitive, or developmental limitations

donate (DOH-nayt) to give money or goods to a person in need or a group working for people in need

inaccessible (ih-nik-SEH-suh-buhl) unable to be reached; blocked

inclusive (in-KLOO-siv) open to everyone, not just to certain people.

independent (in-duh-PEN-duhnt) self-sufficient; able to do things for oneself

FIND OUT MORE

Books

Finke, Beth. *What Is the Americans with Disabilities Act?* Ann Arbor, MI: Cherry Lake Press, 2023.

Hawley, Erin. *Disability Pride.* Ann Arbor, MI: Cherry Lake Press, 2023.

Hawley, Erin. *What Is Disability?* Ann Arbor, MI: Cherry Lake Press, 2023.

Websites

With an adult, find out more online with these suggested searches.

Disability History Museum

Learn more about Homer and Edgar Allen and their legacies.

Easterseals

Explore the programs and services that Easterseals offers in your area and across the country.

Easterseals Disability Film Challenge

Read the film challenge's success stories and find out more about winning projects.

INDEX

ABOUT THE AUTHOR

Beth Finke is blind. She uses a special computer to write. When she types, the computer reads the words out loud. Beth writes books. She wrote four books for children. She wrote two books for grown-ups, too. Her books show readers that people with disabilities can have fun just like other people do. Beth lives in Chicago with her husband Michael and her Seeing Eye dog Luna.